GRAPHIC ORGANIZERS

FOR MATH

IncentivePublications

Written by Marjorie Frank and Jill Norris
Designed and illustrated by Kathleen Bullock

ISBN 978-0-86530-036-1

1   2   3   4   5   6   7   8   9   10   10   09   08   07

PRINTED IN THE UNITED STATES OF AMERICA
www.incentivepublications.com

Using Graphic Organizers

The use of graphic organizers is an important part of many math processes. Students learn to:

- understand ways of representing numbers
- show relationships among numbers
- break apart and analyze each step of math processes
- demonstrate understandings of processes
- communicate math concepts and processes
- visualize patterns and relations
- represent mathematical ideas in a variety of ways
- explain problem-solving strategies

Analysis and communication are critical to all areas of mathematics. The National Council of Teachers of Mathematics encourages the use of diagrams and visuals to help students develop problem-solving abilities. In addition, communication is identified as a key curriculum standard for mathematics. Graphic organizers help students analyze the steps in mathematical thinking and communicate with words, numbers, and symbols each step of their problem-solving process.

Graphic Organizers for Math is one resource every math teacher needs. Here are **47** graphic organizers for guiding the problem-solving process, using various problem-solving processes, and explaining or demonstrating specific math concepts and processes. And that's not all! There are also **nine** pages of checklists, guides, and tips to assist math problem-solvers as they work—including a problem-solving scoring rubric to help evaluate student progress. Use these organizers and tools to spark student thinking and enhance their problem-solving skills.

Help students organize for success!

Graphic Organizers

for

Problem-Solving Approaches and Strategies

Help students understand problem-solving approaches and strategies

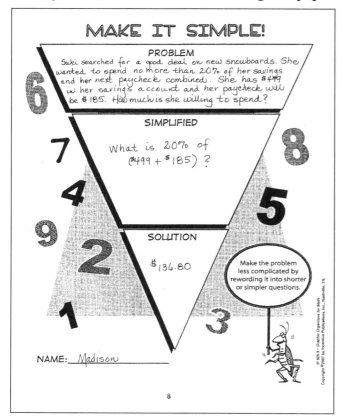

MAKE IT SIMPLE!

PROBLEM

Suki searched for a good deal on new snowboards. She wanted to spend no more than 20% of her savings and her next paycheck combined. She has $499 in her savings account and her paycheck will be $185. How much is she willing to spend?

SIMPLIFIED

What is 20% of ($499 + $185)?

SOLUTION

$136.80

Make the problem less complicated by rewording it into shorter or simpler questions.

NAME: Madison

8

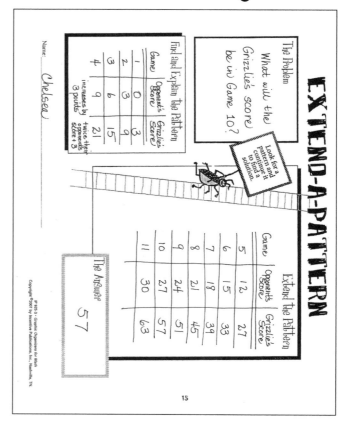

EXTEND-A-PATTERN

Name: Chelsea

The Problem

What will the Grizzlies' score be in Game 10?

Look for a pattern and continue it to find a solution.

Find and Explain the Pattern

Game	Opponent's Score	Grizzlies' Score
1	0	3
2	3	9
3	6	15
4	9	21

increases by 3 points

twice their opponents' score + 3

Extend the Pattern

Game	Opponent's Score	Grizzlies' Score
5	12	27
6	15	33
7	18	39
8	21	45
9	24	51
10	27	57
11	30	63

The Answer

57

15

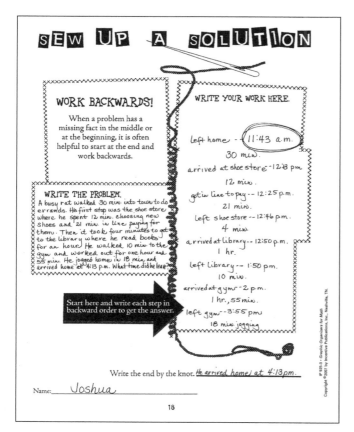

SEW UP A SOLUTION

WORK BACKWARDS!

When a problem has a missing fact in the middle or at the beginning, it is often helpful to start at the end and work backwards.

WRITE THE PROBLEM.

A busy rat walked 30 min. into town to do errands. His first stop was the shoe store where he spent 12 min. choosing new shoes and 21 min. in line paying for them. Then it took four minutes to get to the library where he read books for an hour. He walked 10 min. to the gym and worked out for one hour and 55 min. He jogged home in 18 min. and arrived home at 4:13 p.m. What time did he leave?

Start here and write each step in backward order to get the answer.

WRITE YOUR WORK HERE.

left home — 11:43 a.m.
30 min.
arrived at shoe store — 12:13 pm
12 min.
got in line to pay — 12:25 p.m.
21 min.
left shoe store — 12:46 p.m.
4 min.
arrived at library — 12:50 p.m.
1 hr.
left Library — 1:50 pm
10 min.
arrived at gym — 2 p.m.
1 hr., 55 min.
left gym — 3:55 pm
18 min. jogging

Write the end by the knot. He arrived home at 4:13pm.

Name: Joshua

18

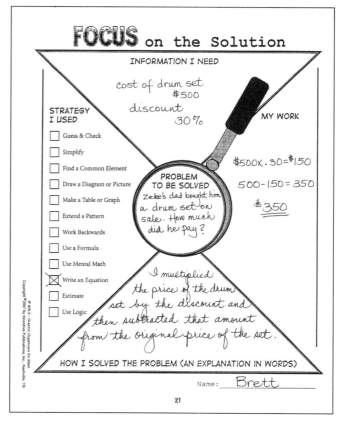

FOCUS on the Solution

INFORMATION I NEED

cost of drum set $500

discount 30%

STRATEGY I USED

- ☐ Guess & Check
- ☐ Simplify
- ☐ Find a Common Element
- ☐ Draw a Diagram or Picture
- ☐ Make a Table or Graph
- ☐ Extend a Pattern
- ☐ Work Backwards
- ☐ Use a Formula
- ☐ Use Mental Math
- ☒ Write an Equation
- ☐ Estimate
- ☐ Use Logic

PROBLEM TO BE SOLVED

Zeke's dad bought him a drum set on sale. How much did he pay?

MY WORK

$500 × .30 = $150

500 − 150 = 350

$350

I multiplied the price of the drum set by the discount and then subtracted that amount from the original price of the set.

HOW I SOLVED THE PROBLEM (AN EXPLANATION IN WORDS)

Name: Brett

21

Before You Begin . . .

1 **What's the Problem?**

Write the question or problem that needs be to solved.

_____
_____
_____
_____

_____
_____
_____
_____
_____

2 **What Information Will Help?**

Write the facts given in the problem that will help you solve it.

3 **What Operation Is Needed?**

Identify one or more operations that will be needed to solve the problem.

_____
_____
_____
_____

4 **What's the Order?**

Explain the order in which the operations must be performed to solve the problem.

Name:_____

IP 925-3 • *Graphic Organizers for Math*
Copyright © 2007 by Incentive Publications, Inc., Nashville, TN.

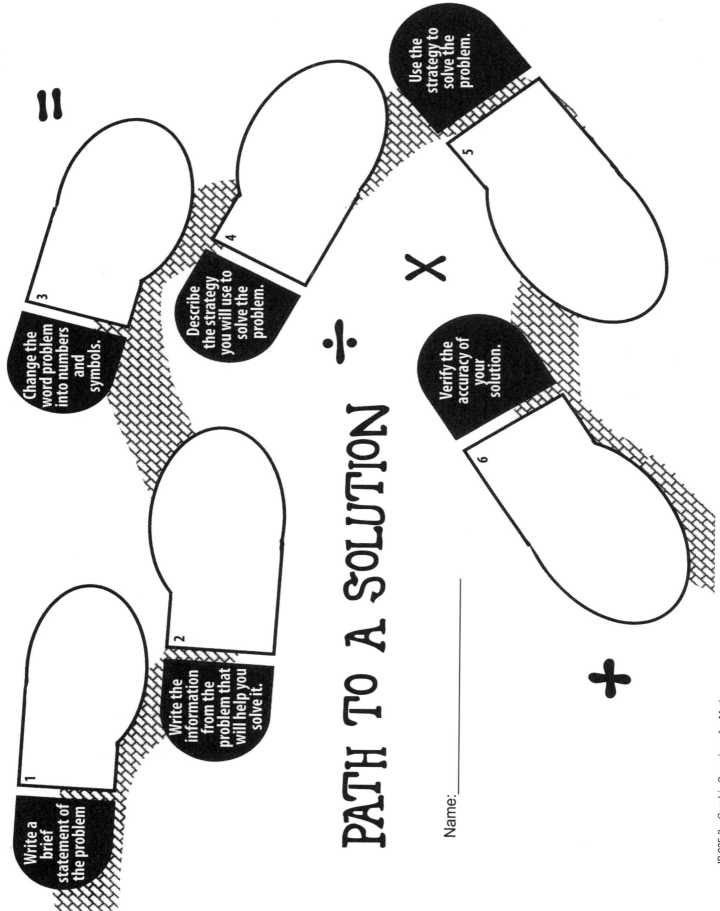

PATH TO A SOLUTION

1 Write a brief statement of the problem

2 Write the information from the problem that will help you solve it.

3 Change the word problem into numbers and symbols.

4 Describe the strategy you will use to solve the problem.

5 Use the strategy to solve the problem.

6 Verify the accuracy of your solution.

Name: _____

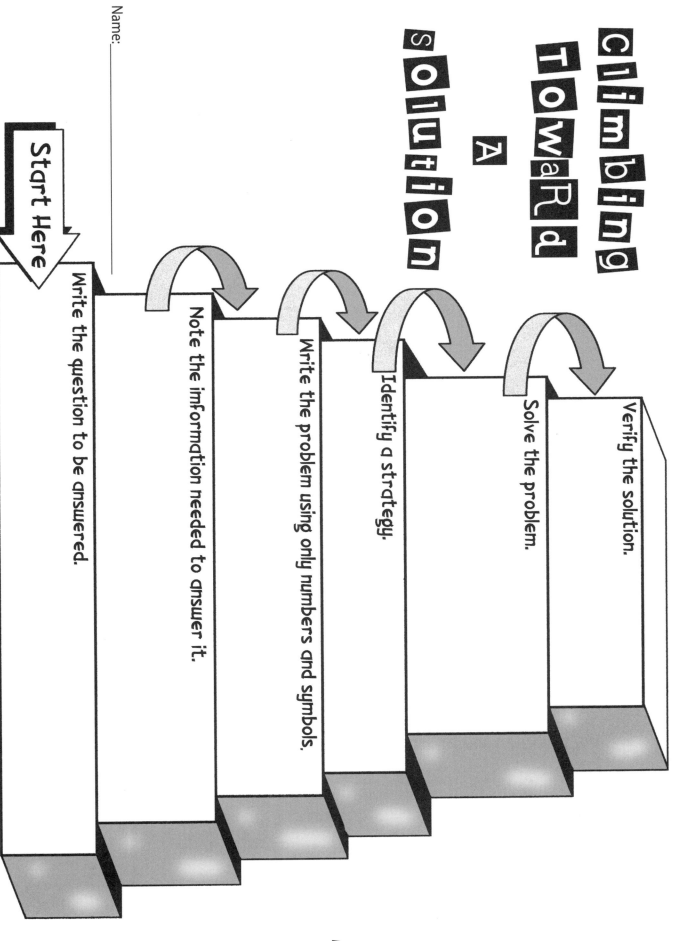

Climbing Toward a Solution

Name: _____

Start Here

Write the question to be answered.

Note the information needed to answer it.

Write the problem using only numbers and symbols.

Identify a strategy.

Solve the problem.

Verify the solution.

MAKE IT SIMPLE!

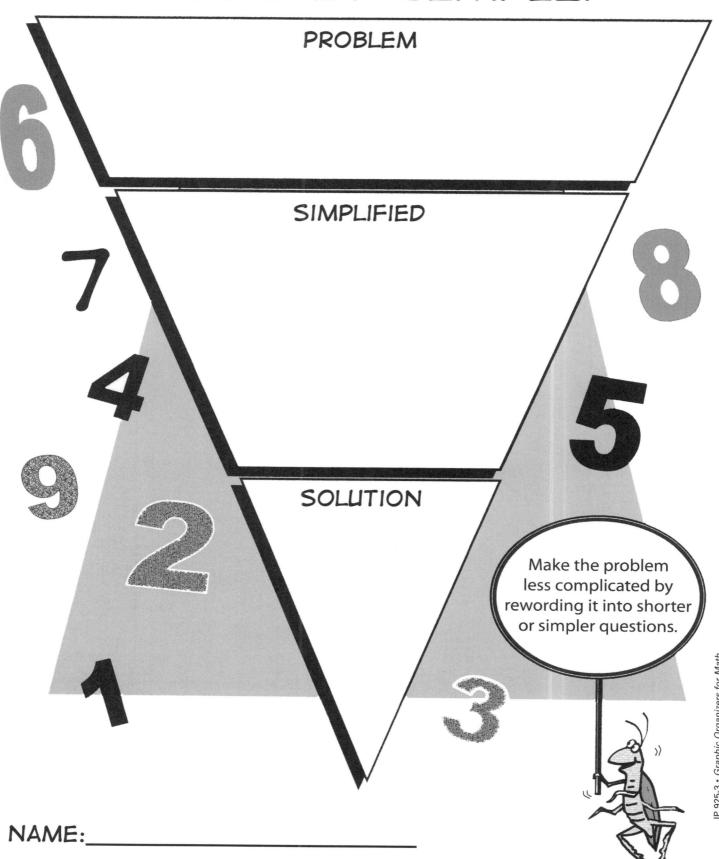

PROBLEM

6

SIMPLIFIED

7   8

4   5

9

2

SOLUTION

1   3

Make the problem less complicated by rewording it into shorter or simpler questions.

NAME:_____

IP 925-3 • *Graphic Organizers for Math*
Copyright ©2007 by Incentive Publications, Inc., Nashville, TN.

Guess & Check

Make a careful guess, then count or calculate to see if it was right. Keep trying different solutions until you find one that's right.

The Problem

Guess

Check

Guess

Check

Guess

Check

Guess

Check

The Answer

How many guesses did it take?

Name:_____

IP 925-3 • *Graphic Organizers for Math*
Copyright © 2007 by Incentive Publications, Inc., Nashville, TN.

Name:_____

The Problem

Round, Estimate, & Check

Rounded Numbers

My Estimated Answer

Calculation

The Actual Answer

How Close Did I Come?

When you need an approximate answer, the best strategy is estimation.

IP 925-3 • Graphic Organizers for Math
Copyright ©2007 by Incentive Publications, Inc., Nashville, TN.

BRIGHT IDEAS

Tell how you used mental math to solve the problem.

The Problem

The Solution

Name:_____

IP 925-3 • *Graphic Organizers for Math*
Copyright ©2007 by Incentive Publications, Inc., Nashville, TN.

FOLLOW THE FORMULA

The Problem

The Formula

Use the right formula!

Your Work

Whenever you can, use a formula as the shortcut to a solution.

The Solution

Name:_____

Display the Data

The Problem

Make a table or graph to show the data.

The Solution

Name:_____

Picture It!

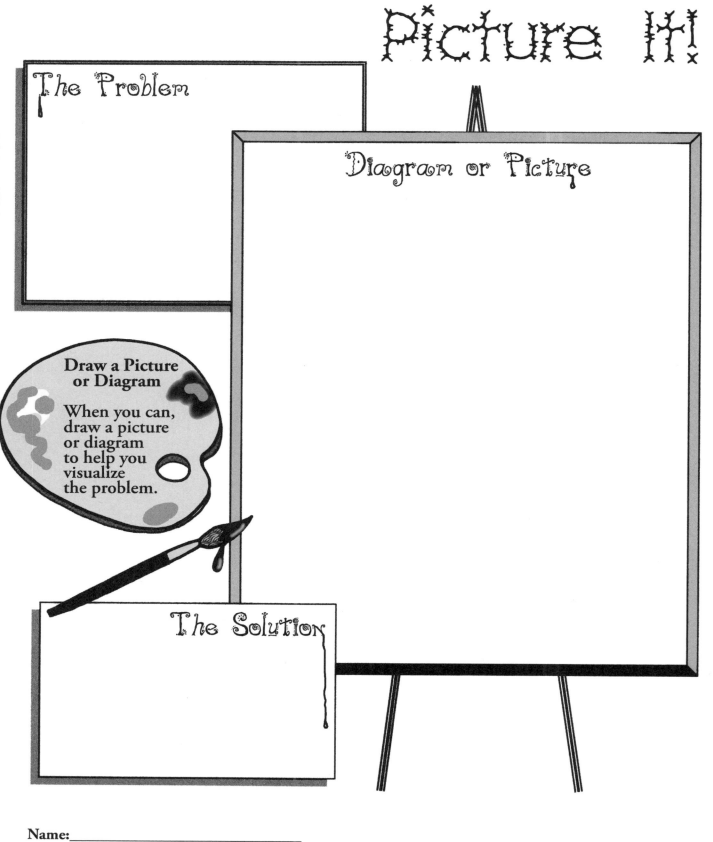

The Problem

Diagram or Picture

Draw a Picture or Diagram

When you can, draw a picture or diagram to help you visualize the problem.

The Solution

Name:_____

IP 925-3 • *Graphic Organizers for Math*

Name: _____

EXTEND A PATTERN

The Problem

Find and Explain the Pattern

Look for a pattern and continue it to find a solution.

Extend the Pattern

The Answer

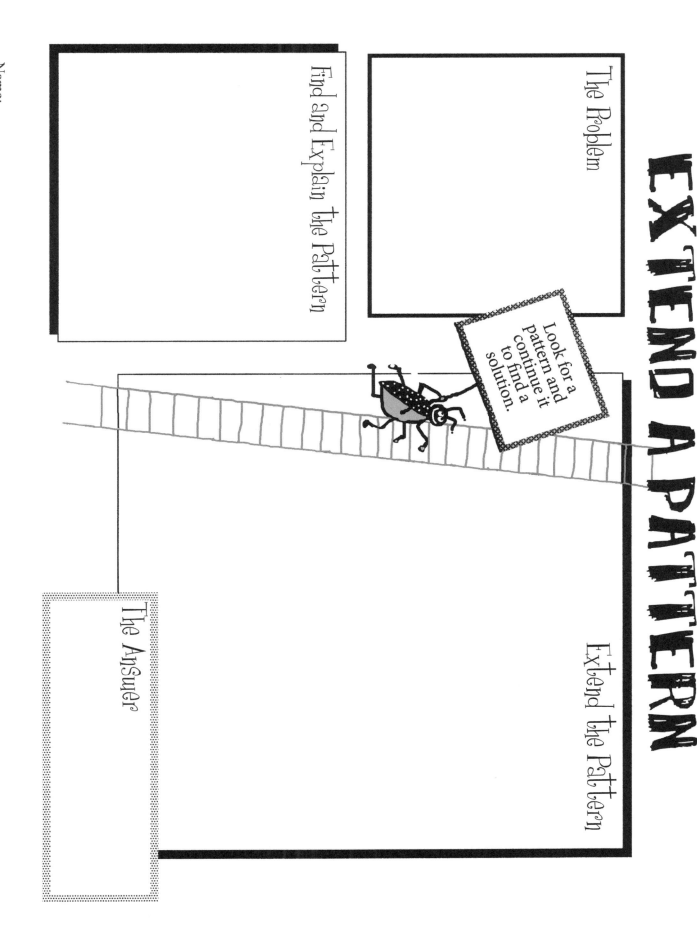

IP 925-3 • *Graphic Organizers for Math*
Copyright © 2007 by Incentive Publications, Inc., Nashville, TN.

Unlock the Problem

The Problem

The Key

The Common Element

The Solution

Find a Common Element

If the facts in a problem include different units, convert all the information into the same unit.

Name:_____

IP 925-3 • *Graphic Organizers for Math*
Copyright ©2007 by Incentive Publications, Inc., Nashville, TN.

QUICK CHANGE

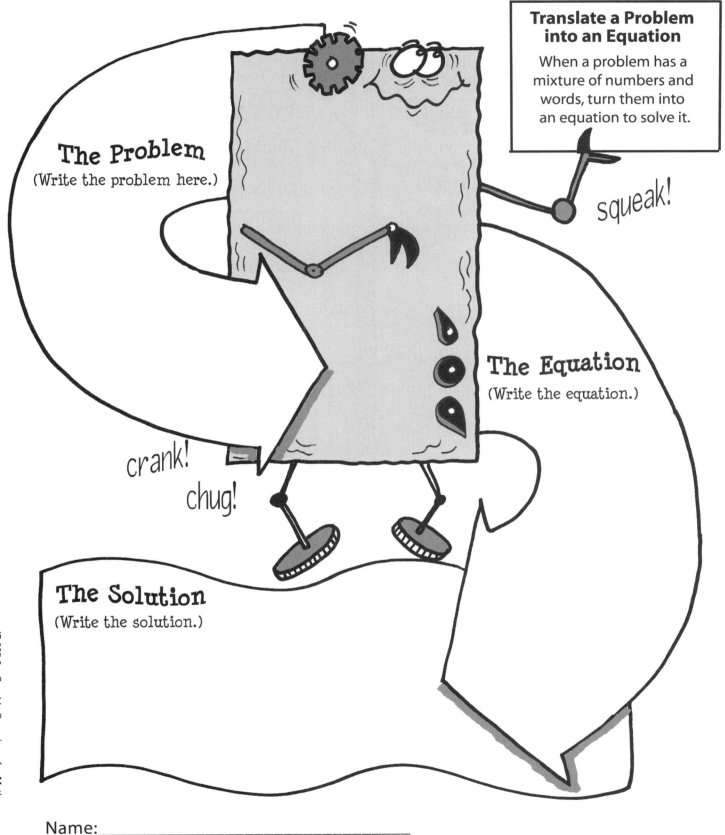

Translate a Problem into an Equation

When a problem has a mixture of numbers and words, turn them into an equation to solve it.

The Problem
(Write the problem here.)

squeak!

The Equation
(Write the equation.)

crank!

chug!

The Solution
(Write the solution.)

IP 925-3 • *Graphic Organizers for Math*
Copyright © 2007 by Incentive Publications, Inc., Nashville, TN.

Name:_____

SEW UP A SOLUTION

WORK BACKWARDS!

When a problem has a missing fact in the middle or at the beginning, it is often helpful to start at the end and work backwards.

WRITE YOUR WORK HERE.

WRITE THE PROBLEM.

Start here and write each step in backward order to get the answer.

Write the end by the knot. _____

Name: _____

IP 925-3 • Graphic Organizers for Math
Copyright ©2007 by Incentive Publications, Inc., Nashville, TN.

Two Ways to Go!

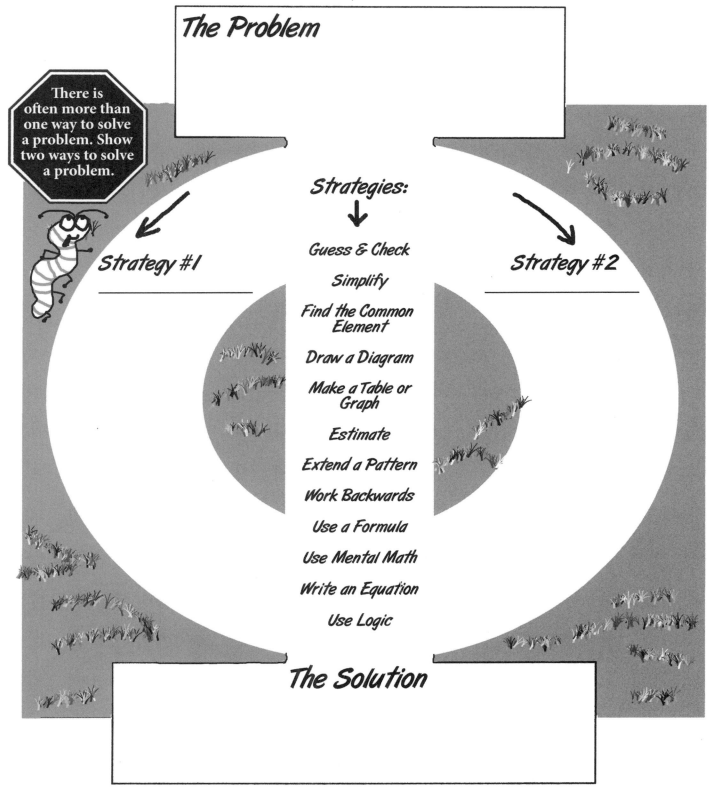

The Problem

There is often more than one way to solve a problem. Show two ways to solve a problem.

Strategy #1

Strategies:

Guess & Check

Simplify

Find the Common Element

Draw a Diagram

Make a Table or Graph

Estimate

Extend a Pattern

Work Backwards

Use a Formula

Use Mental Math

Write an Equation

Use Logic

Strategy #2

The Solution

Name:_____

IP 925-3 • *Graphic Organizers for Math*
Copyright © 2007 by Incentive Publications, Inc., Nashville, TN.

MORE THAN ONE SOLUTION

Solution #1

Solution #2

Solution #3

The Problem

Some problems have more than one possible correct solution. Find three solutions for the problem.

Name:_____

IP 925-3 • *Graphic Organizers for Math*
Copyright ©2007 by Incentive Publications, Inc., Nashville, TN.

FOCUS on the Solution

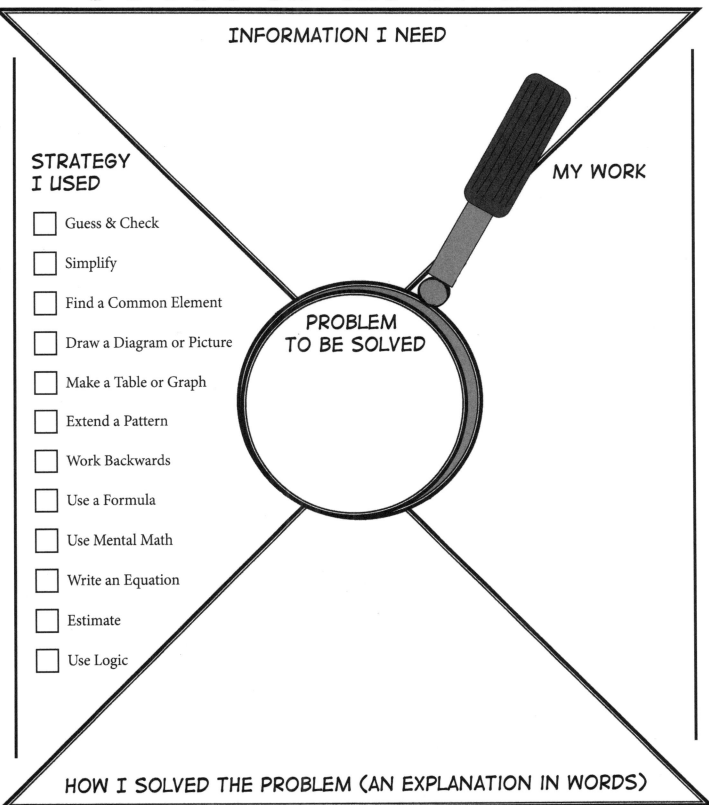

INFORMATION I NEED

STRATEGY
I USED

☐ Guess & Check

☐ Simplify

☐ Find a Common Element

☐ Draw a Diagram or Picture

☐ Make a Table or Graph

☐ Extend a Pattern

☐ Work Backwards

☐ Use a Formula

☐ Use Mental Math

☐ Write an Equation

☐ Estimate

☐ Use Logic

MY WORK

PROBLEM
TO BE SOLVED

HOW I SOLVED THE PROBLEM (AN EXPLANATION IN WORDS)

Name: _____

IP 925-3 • *Graphic Organizers for Math*
Copyright © 2007 by Incentive Publications, Inc., Nashville, TN.

WORDS AND NUMBERS

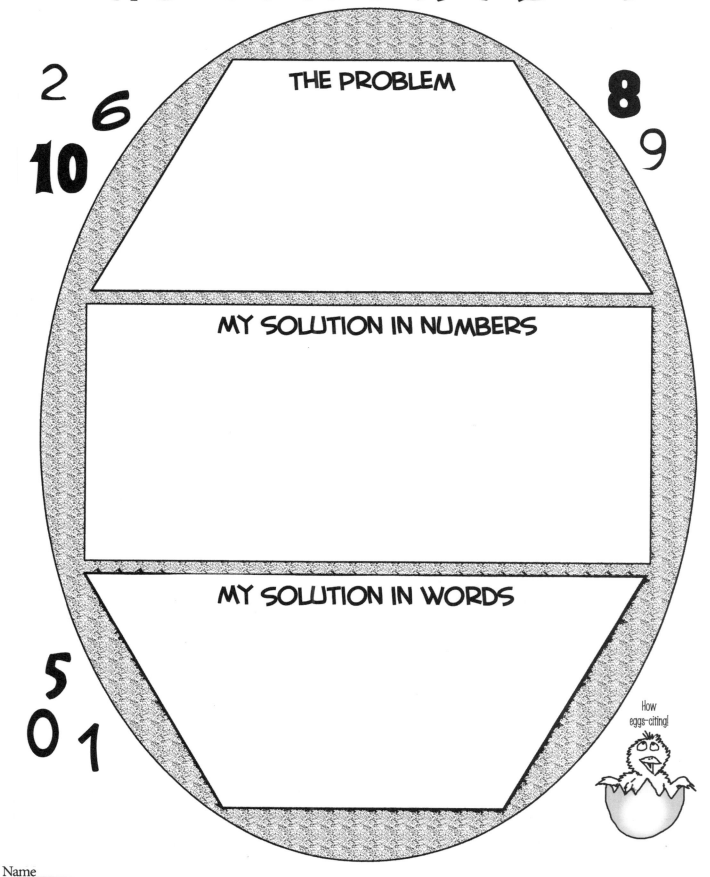

2 6 8
10 9

THE PROBLEM

MY SOLUTION IN NUMBERS

MY SOLUTION IN WORDS

5
0 1

How eggs-citing!

IP 925-3 • *Graphic Organizers for Math*
Copyright ©2007 by Incentive Publications, Inc., Nashville, TN.

Name_____

PUZZLE A SOLUTION

SOLVE THE PROBLEM STEP BY STEP. EXPLAIN WHAT YOU DID IN EACH STEP.

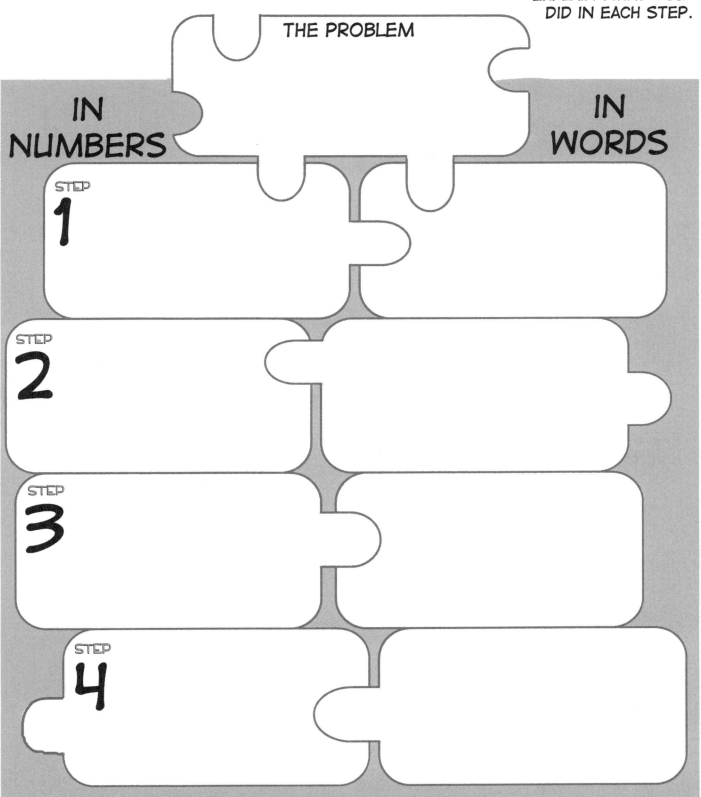

THE PROBLEM

IN NUMBERS

IN WORDS

STEP 1

STEP 2

STEP 3

STEP 4

IP 925-3 • *Graphic Organizers for Math*
Copyright ©2007 by Incentive Publications, Inc., Nashville, TN.

NAME:_____

Double-Check

Write the problem.

Solve the problem.

Verify the solution.

Name:_____

24

IP 925-3 • *Graphic Organizers for Math*

Graphic Organizers

for

Explanations of
Math Concepts and Processes

Use graphic organizers
to explain math concepts and processes

FLIP IT!

Show the process for dividing fractions.

$$\frac{8}{12} \div \frac{3}{4} = \frac{8}{12} \times \frac{4}{3} = \frac{32}{36} \text{ or } \frac{8}{9}$$

$$\frac{6}{7} \div \frac{2}{3} = \frac{6}{7} \times \frac{3}{2} = \frac{18}{14} \text{ or } 1\frac{2}{7}$$

$$\frac{5}{8} \div \frac{1}{3} = \frac{5}{8} \times \frac{3}{1} = \frac{15}{8} \text{ or } 1\frac{7}{8}$$

$$\frac{2}{5} \div \frac{3}{4} = \frac{2}{5} \times \frac{4}{3} = \frac{8}{15}$$

$$\frac{7}{8} \div \frac{3}{7} = \frac{7}{8} \times \frac{7}{3} = \frac{49}{24} \text{ or } 2\frac{1}{24}$$

Name: Matt

30

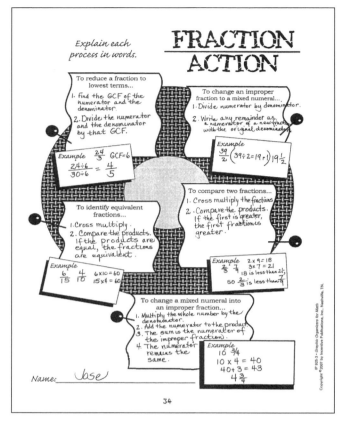

FRACTION ACTION

Explain each process in words.

To reduce a fraction to lowest terms...
1. find the GCF of the numerator and the denominator.
2. Divide the numerator and the denominator by that GCF.

Example $\frac{24}{30}$ GCF=6
$\frac{24 \div 6}{30 \div 6} = \frac{4}{5}$

To change an improper fraction to a mixed numeral...
1. Divide numerator by denominator.
2. Write any remainder as a numerator of a new fraction with the original denominator.

Example $\frac{39}{2}$ $(39 \div 2 = 19 \, r \, 1)$ $19\frac{1}{2}$

To identify equivalent fractions...
1. Cross multiply.
2. Compare the products. If the products are equal, the fractions are equivalent.

Example $\frac{6}{15} \quad \frac{4}{10}$ $6 \times 10 = 60$ $15 \times 4 = 60$

To compare two fractions...
1. Cross multiply the fractions.
2. Compare the products. If the first is greater, the first fraction is greater.

Example $\frac{2}{3} \quad \frac{7}{9}$ $2 \times 9 = 18$ $3 \times 7 = 21$ 18 is less than 21, so $\frac{2}{3}$ is less than $\frac{7}{9}$

To change a mixed numeral into an improper fraction...
1. Multiply the whole number by the denominator.
2. Add the numerator to the product.
3. The sum is the numerator of the improper fraction.
4. The numerator remains the same.

Example $10\frac{3}{4}$
$10 \times 4 = 40$
$40 + 3 = 43$
$\frac{43}{4}$

Name: Jose

34

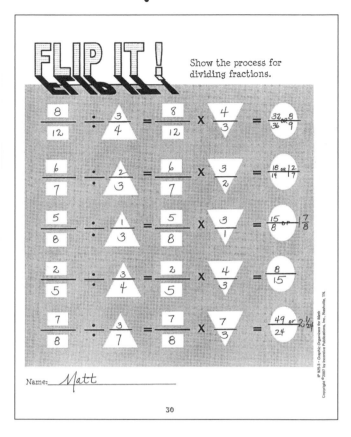

How Do You Know?

Finish each explanation.

A number is divisible by **2** if... the last digit is 0, 2, 4, 6, or 8.
Examples 98, 4, 6,236

A number is divisible by **3** if... the sum of its digits is divisible by 3.
Examples 33, 921

A number is divisible by **9** if... the sum of its digits is divisible by 9.
Examples 468, 504, 1,134

A number is divisible by **8** if... the number formed by the last three digits is divisible by 8.
Examples 3,170,576, 7,416

A number is divisible by **4** if... the number formed by the last two digits is divisible by 4.
Examples 35,192, 516, 6,124,012

A number is divisible by **7** if... There is no easy test!
Examples 49, 2,464

A number is divisible by **6** if..... the number is divisible by both 2 and 3.
Examples 36, 654, 924

A number is divisible by **5** if.... the last digit is 0 or 5.
Examples 40, 3,025, 1,262,340

Divisibility

Name: Amy

37

FUNCTION TABLES

Rule: Output = $\frac{Input}{5}$
Explain the Rule: Divide the number in first column by 5.

30	6
40	8
50	10
65	13

Rule: Output = Input − 8
Explain the Rule: Subtract 8 from the number in column one.

−6	−14
−1	−9
4	−4
8	0

Rule: Output = Input − 2
Explain the Rule: Subtract 2 from the input (column one)

0	−2
31	29
9	7
7	5

Rule: m = 7 h
Explain the Rule: Multiply input (h) by 7 to get output (m)

1	7
2	14
3	21
4	28

Rule: y = x + 3
Explain the Rule: Add 3 to input (x) to get output (y).

2	5
−1	2
0	3
1	4

Rule: Output = Input (−2)
Explain the Rule: Multiply input by a negative two.

1	2
1	−2
3	−6
−2	4

Rule: y = 2x + 1
Explain the Rule: Multiply input (x) by 2 and add 1.

3	7
5	11
7	15
9	19

NAME: Vinnie

38

DEFINITIONS IN THE BAG!

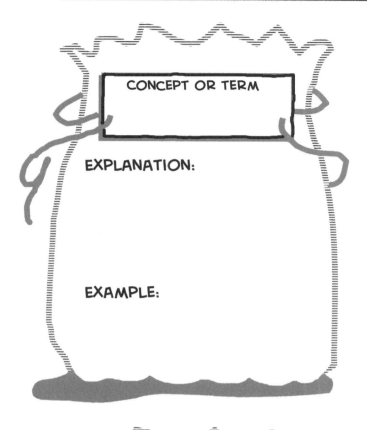

CONCEPT OR TERM

EXPLANATION:

EXAMPLE:

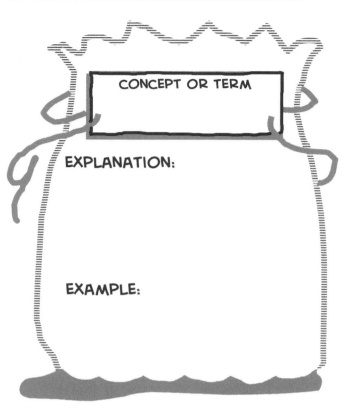

CONCEPT OR TERM

EXPLANATION:

EXAMPLE:

CONCEPT OR TERM

EXPLANATION:

EXAMPLE:

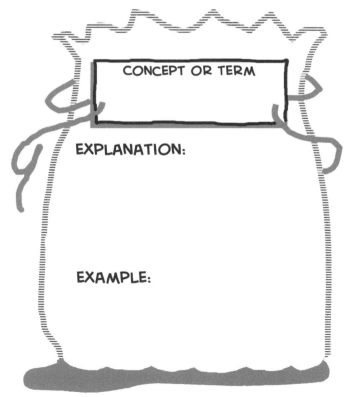

CONCEPT OR TERM

EXPLANATION:

EXAMPLE:

NAME:_____

IP 925-3 • *Graphic Organizers for Math*
Copyright © 2007 by Incentive Publications, Inc., Nashville, TN.

Hot Properties!

Explanation in words:

Show an example:

Property

Explanation in words:

Show an example:

Property

Explanation in words:

Show an example:

Property

Name: _____

IP 925-3 • *Graphic Organizers for Math*
Copyright ©2007 by Incentive Publications, Inc., Nashville, TN.

MAKING CHANGES

HOW TO CHANGE A DECIMAL TO A FRACTION:

EXPLAIN
THE PROCESS
IN WORDS.

HOW TO CHANGE A FRACTION TO A DECIMAL:

HOW TO CHANGE A DECIMAL TO A PERCENT:

HOW TO CHANGE A PERCENT TO A DECIMAL:

NAME:_____

IP 925-3 • *Graphic Organizers for Math*
Copyright © 2007 by Incentive Publications, Inc., Nashville, TN.

FLIP IT !

Show the process for dividing fractions.

Name: _____

IP 925-3 • *Graphic Organizers for Math*
Copyright ©2007 by Incentive Publications, Inc., Nashville, TN.

Precise Percentages

Example:_____

Step 1.

Step 2.

How to Find a Percentage of a Number

Show an example, then explain the steps in words.

How to Tell What Percent One Number is of Another

Show an example, then explain the steps in words.

Example:_____

Step 1.

Step 2.

How to Find the Base When You Know the Percent

Show an example, then explain the steps in words.

Example:_____

Step 1.

Step 2.

Name:_____

Keep It Balanced

Solve the Equation.
Show each step.

The Equation

The Solution

Name: _____

IP 925-3 • *Graphic Organizers for Math*
Copyright ©2007 by Incentive Publications, Inc., Nashville, TN.

How To Do It

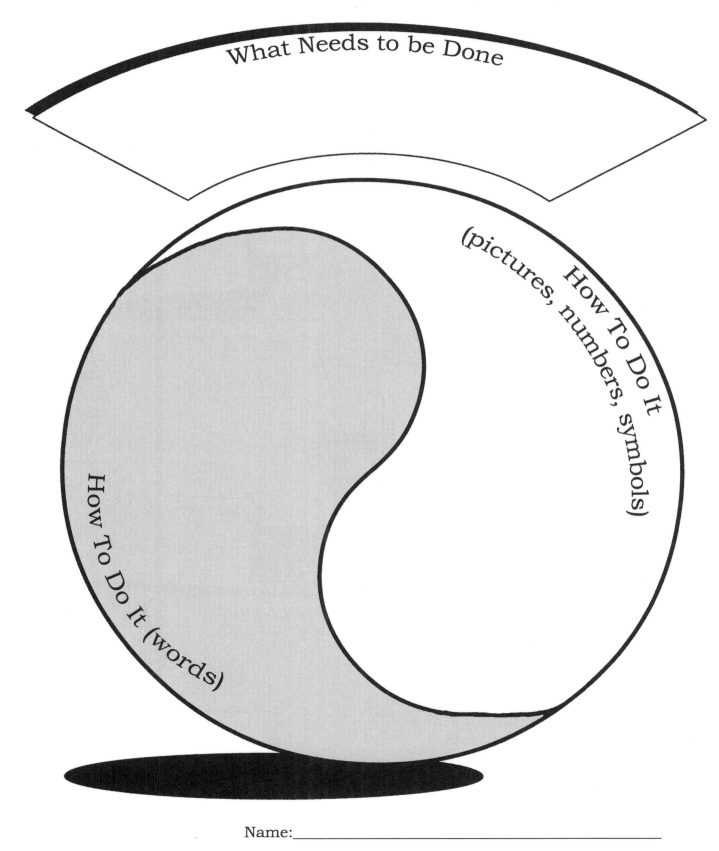

What Needs to be Done

How To Do It (pictures, numbers, symbols)

How To Do It (words)

Name:_____

IP 925-3 • *Graphic Organizers for Math*
Copyright © 2007 by Incentive Publications, Inc., Nashville, TN.

Explain each process in words.

FRACTION ACTION

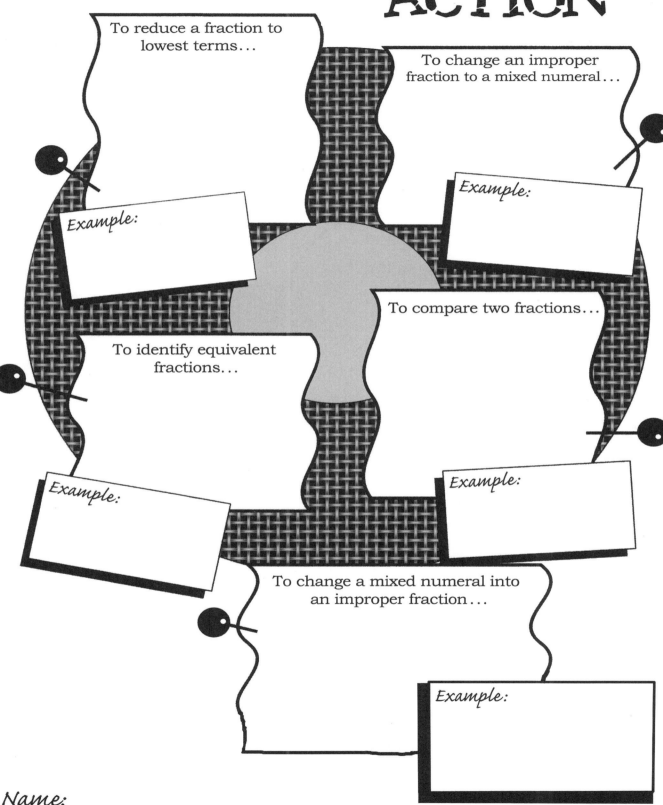

To reduce a fraction to lowest terms…

To change an improper fraction to a mixed numeral…

Example:

Example:

To compare two fractions…

To identify equivalent fractions…

Example:

Example:

To change a mixed numeral into an improper fraction…

Example:

Name:_____

IP 925-3 • *Graphic Organizers for Math*
Copyright ©2007 by Incentive Publications, Inc., Nashville, TN.

TAXES & Tips

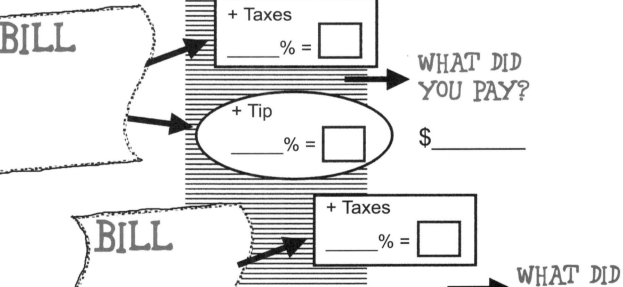

BILL

+ Taxes

_____ % = ☐

+ Tip

_____ % = ☐

WHAT DID YOU PAY?

$_____

BILL

+ Taxes

_____ % = ☐

+ Tip

_____ % = ☐

WHAT DID YOU PAY?

$_____

BILL

+ Taxes

_____ % = ☐

+ Tip

_____ % = ☐

WHAT DID YOU PAY?

$_____

BILL

+ Taxes

_____ % = ☐

+ Tip

_____ % = ☐

WHAT DID YOU PAY?

$_____

IP 925-3 • Graphic Organizers for Math
Copyright © 2007 by Incentive Publications, Inc., Nashville, TN.

Name:_____

EXPLAIN IT TO LEARN IT!

Explain each process in words.

 cube

How to find volume:

How to find surface area:

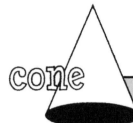 cone

How to find volume:

How to find surface area:

 cylinder

How to find volume:

How to find surface area:

 sphere

How to find volume:

How to find surface area:

 prism

How to find volume:

How to find surface area:

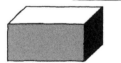 pyramid

How to find volume:

How to find surface area:

Name: _____

IP 925-3 • *Graphic Organizers for Math*
Copyright ©2007 by Incentive Publications, Inc., Nashville, TN.

How Do You Know?

Finish each explanation.

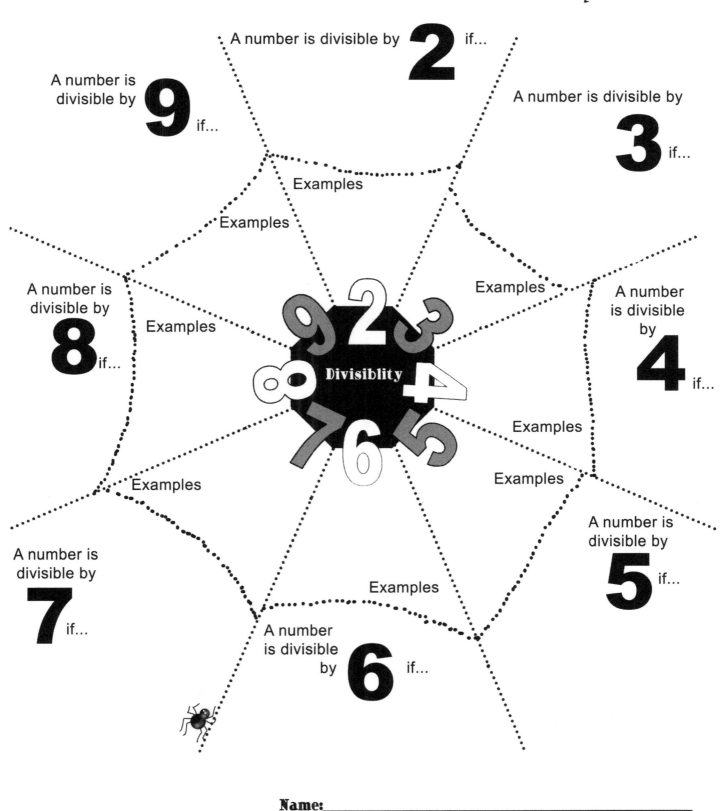

A number is divisible by **2** if...

A number is divisible by **3** if...

A number is divisible by **9** if...

A number is divisible by **8** if...

A number is divisible by **4** if...

A number is divisible by **5** if...

A number is divisible by **7** if...

A number is divisible by **6** if...

Examples

Examples

Examples

Examples

Examples

Examples

Examples

Examples

Divisiblity

Name:_____

IP 925-3 • *Graphic Organizers for Math*
Copyright ©2007 by Incentive Publications, Inc., Nashville, TN.

FUNCTION TABLES

Rule:
_____
Explain the Rule:
_____
_____

Rule:
_____
Explain the Rule:
_____
_____

Rule:
_____
Explain the Rule:
_____
_____

Rule:
_____
Explain the Rule:
_____
_____

Rule:
_____
Explain the Rule:
_____
_____

Rule:
_____
Explain the Rule:
_____
_____

Rule:
_____
Explain the Rule:
_____
_____

NAME:_____

IP 925-3 • *Graphic Organizers for Math*
Copyright © 2007 by Incentive Publications, Inc., Nashville, TN.

FIGURE THIS!

NAME IT. **SHOW IT.** **DESCRIBE IT.**

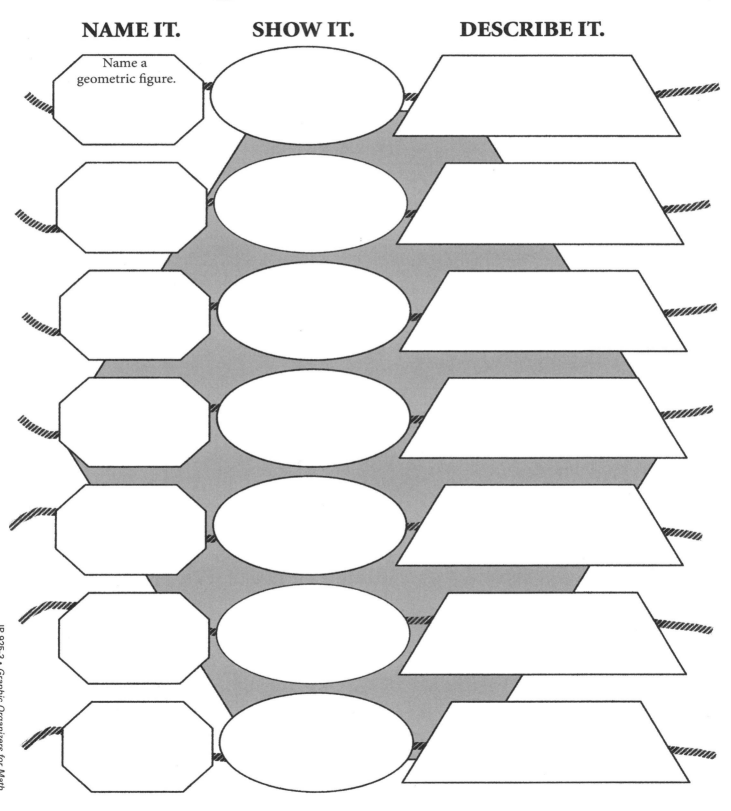

Name a geometric figure.

Name:_____

IP 925-3 • *Graphic Organizers for Math*
Copyright © 2007 by Incentive Publications, Inc., Nashville, TN.

Fission Factors

WRITE NUMBERS IN
THE CIRCLES.

WRITE FACTORS ON THE LINES.
_____

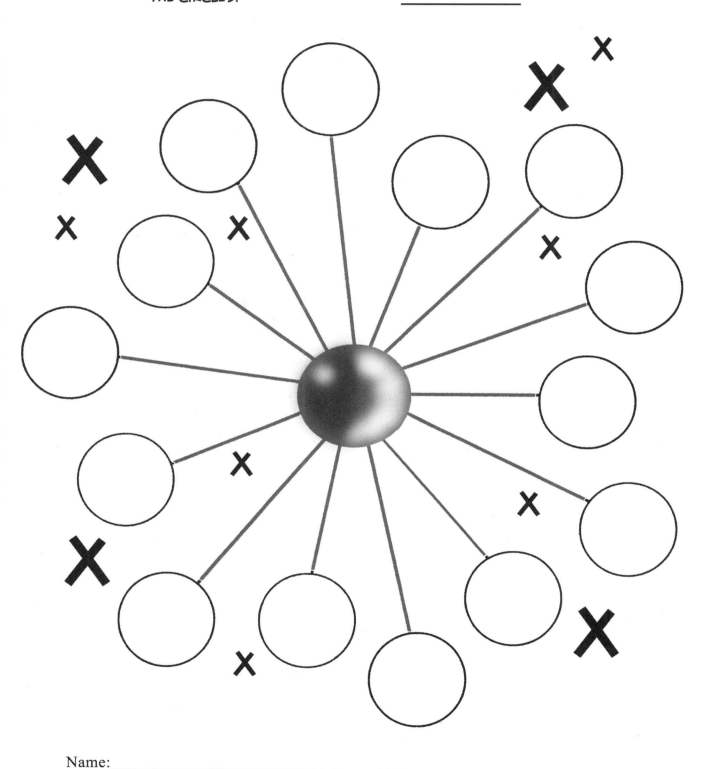

Name:_____

IP 925-3 • *Graphic Organizers for Math*

Tools, Tips, & More
Graphic Organizers

Provide the organizers students need
to do math homework successfully

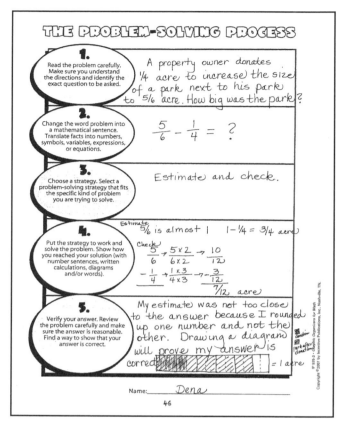

THE PROBLEM-SOLVING PROCESS

1. Read the problem carefully. Make sure you understand the directions and identify the exact question to be asked.

A property owner donates ¼ acre to increase the size of a park next to his park to ⅚ acre. How big was the park?

2. Change the word problem into a mathematical sentence. Translate facts into numbers, symbols, variables, expressions, or equations.

$$\frac{5}{6} - \frac{1}{4} = ?$$

3. Choose a strategy. Select a problem-solving strategy that fits the specific kind of problem you are trying to solve.

Estimate and check.

4. Put the strategy to work and solve the problem. Show how you reached your solution (with number sentences, written calculations, diagrams and/or words).

Estimate ⅚ is almost 1   1 - ¼ = ¾ acre

Check
$$\frac{5}{6} \rightarrow \frac{5 \times 2}{6 \times 2} \rightarrow \frac{10}{12}$$
$$-\frac{1}{4} \rightarrow \frac{1 \times 3}{4 \times 3} \rightarrow -\frac{3}{12}$$
$$\frac{7}{12} \text{ acre}$$

5. Verify your answer. Review the problem carefully and make sure the answer is reasonable. Find a way to show that your answer is correct.

My estimate was not too close to the answer because I rounded up one number and not the other. Drawing a diagram will prove my answer is correct.   = 1 acre

Name: Dena
46

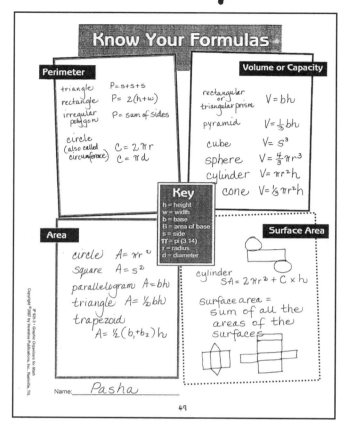

Know Your Formulas

Perimeter

triangle	$P = s+s+s$
rectangle	$P = 2(h+w)$
irregular polygon	$P = $ sum of sides
circle (also called circumference)	$C = 2\pi r$ $C = \pi d$

Volume or Capacity

rectangular or triangular prism	$V = bh$
pyramid	$V = \frac{1}{3}bh$
cube	$V = s^3$
sphere	$V = \frac{4}{3}\pi r^3$
cylinder	$V = \pi r^2 h$
cone	$V = \frac{1}{3}\pi r^2 h$

Key
h = height
w = width
b = base
B = area of base
s = side
π = pi (3.14)
r = radius
d = diameter

Area

circle	$A = \pi r^2$
square	$A = s^2$
parallelogram	$A = bh$
triangle	$A = \frac{1}{2}bh$
trapezoid	$A = \frac{1}{2}(b_1 + b_2)h$

Surface Area

cylinder $SA = 2\pi r^2 + C \times h$

Surface area = sum of all the areas of the surfaces

Name: Pasha
49

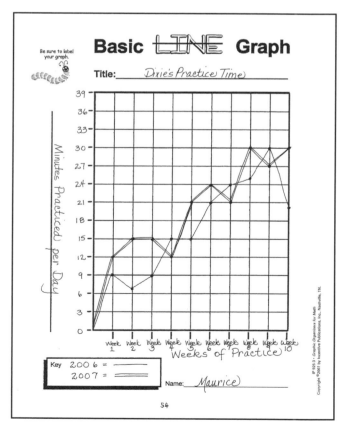

Be sure to label your graph.

Basic LINE Graph

Title: Dixie's Practice Time

Minutes Practiced per Day (vertical axis: 0, 3, 6, 9, 12, 15, 18, 21, 24, 27, 30, 33, 36, 39)

Weeks of Practice (horizontal axis: Week 1, Week 2, Week 3, Week 4, Week 5, Week 6, Week 7, Week 8, Week 9, Week 10)

Key 2006 = _____
     2007 = _____

Name: Maurice
54

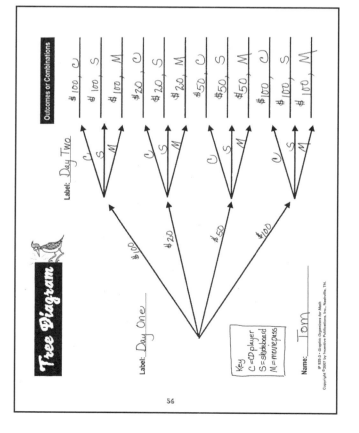

Tree Diagram

Label: Day Two

Outcomes or Combinations:
$100, C
$100, S
$100, M
$20, C
$20, S
$20, M
$50, C
$50, S
$50, M
$100, C
$100, S
$100, M

$100 $20 $50 $100

Label: Day One

Key
C = CD player
S = skateboard
M = movie pass

Name: Tom
56

✔ Checklist of Problem-Solving Strategies

Guess & Check
Start by making a smart guess. Then count or calculate to see if your guess was correct.

Estimate
For a quick approximate solution, round the numbers in a problem and estimate the answer.

Trial & Error
Try out different solutions until you find one that works.

Extend a Pattern
Look for a pattern in the information given, then continue the pattern to find a solution.

Simplify
Make the problem less complicated by rewording it into a shorter or simpler question.

Work Backwards
Start at the end of a problem and work backwards to find the missing fact.

Find a Common Element
Convert different units in a problem to the same unit, preferably the smallest unit.

Use a Formula
Choose the correct formula and use it accurately to find a shortcut to the solution.

Make a Model
Use real materials (such as paper, toothpicks, boxes) to build a model and actually see the object.

Use Mental Math
Think through a problem and come up with a solution without using any tool except your brain.

Draw a Diagram
Draw a diagram or picture to help visualize the situation in the problem.

Write an Equation
Translate the information in a problem into an equation. Then solve it.

Make a Table or Graph
Put data into a table or graph to easily see the relationships between numbers.

Use Logic
Sometimes further information is needed. To make assumptions, use "if/then" reasoning.

IP 925-3 • *Graphic Organizers for Math*
Copyright © 2007 by Incentive Publications, Inc., Nashville, TN.

Clues to Operations

Addition

sum

total   together

add up to

increased by

in all

all together

both

Subtraction

difference   decreased by

"change" in money   take away   remain

left over

less than   how much

more or less

fewer than

Multiplication

how many times

a product of

multiplied by

twice as much as

Division

SPLIT UP   DIVIDED BY

WHAT IS THE AVERAGE   EQUAL PARTS

SHARING   HALF AS MUCH

PARTS

EQUALLY DISTRIBUTED

FRACTIONS

Watch for these words in problems. They are clues to the operation needed to solve the problem.

IP 925-3 • *Graphic Organizers for Math*

Name:_____

RECIPE FOR PROBLEM SOLVING

1. Read the directions twice.

2. Read the problem carefully.

3. Decide exactly what you need to find out.

4. Figure out what information is necessary to solve the problem.

5. Decide on the operation(s) needed.

6. Choose a strategy that fits the problem.

7. Calculate, draw, scratch, doodle, or diagram. Do whatever it takes to figure out the answer.

8. Look closely at the answer. Does it make sense? Is it accurate?

Name:_____

RECIPE FOR PROBLEM SOLVING

1. Read the directions twice.

2. Read the problem carefully.

3. Decide exactly what you need to find out.

4. Figure out what information is necessary to solve the problem.

5. Decide on the operation(s) needed.

6. Choose a strategy that fits the problem.

7. Calculate, draw, scratch, doodle, or diagram. Do whatever it takes to figure out the answer.

8. Look closely at the answer. Does it make sense? Is it accurate?

Name:_____

IP 925-3 • Graphic Organizers for Math
Copyright ©2007 by Incentive Publications, Inc., Nashville, TN.

THE PROBLEM-SOLVING PROCESS

1.
Read the problem carefully. Make sure you understand the directions and identify the exact question to be asked.

2.
Change the word problem into a mathematical sentence. Translate facts into numbers, symbols, variables, expressions, or equations.

3.
Choose a strategy. Select a problem-solving strategy that fits the specific kind of problem you are trying to solve.

4.
Put the strategy to work and solve the problem. Show how you reached your solution (with number sentences, written calculations, diagrams and words).

5.
Verify your answer. Review the problem carefully and make sure the answer is reasonable. Find a way to show that your answer is correct.

IP 925-3 • *Graphic Organizers for Math*
Copyright ©2007 by Incentive Publications, Inc., Nashville, TN.

Name:_____

TIPS FOR SOLVING WORD PROBLEMS

1. Read through the problem twice. Identify the question to be answered. Underline it.

2. Circle key facts needed to solve the problem.

3. Circle clue words that point to the correct operation.

4. Draw pictures or diagrams if you need them.

5. After you find the answer, read the problem again to see that you have answered the question.

6. Check your answer using another method or strategy.

1. Read the number sentence twice.

2. Identify the missing element or number that you need to find.

3. Simplify the sentence by doing the easy computations and by combining elements that are the same.

4. Identify the operation(s) needed to solve the problem. Follow the correct order of operations.

5. Solve the problem.

6. Take your answer and write it into the number sentence or equation.

7. Read the problem again to make sure it is correct with your answer inserted.

TIPS FOR SOLVING NUMBER SENTENCES OR EQUATIONS

PROBLEM-SOLVING RUBRIC

Trait	Expert Problem Solver	Developing Problem Solver	Beginning Problem Solver
Conceptual Understanding			
Strategies & Processes			
Communication			
Correctness (Accuracy of Answers)			
Verification			

Name: _____

IP 925-3 • *Graphic Organizers for Math*
Copyright ©2007 by Incentive Publications, Inc., Nashville, TN.

Know Your Formulas

Perimeter

Volume or Capacity

Key

h = height
w = width
b = base
B = area of base
s = side
π = pi (3.14)
r = radius
d = diameter

Area

Surface Area

Name:_____

GET THE FACTS STRAIGHT

Fill in the missing facts. Then use the grid to help with your math homework.

+	1	2	3	4	5	6	7	8	9	10	11	12	13	14	15
1															
2															
3															
4															
5															
6															
7															
8															
9															
10															
11															
12															
13															
14															
15															

Name:

IP 925-3 • *Graphic Organizers for Math*

Copyright ©2007 by Incentive Publications, Inc., Nashville, TN.

GET THE FACTS STRAIGHT

Fill in the missing facts. Then use the grid to help with your math homework.

x	1	2	3	4	5	6	7	8	9	10	11	12	13	14	15
1															
2															
3															
4															
5															
6															
7															
8															
9															
10															
11															
12															
13															
14															
15															

Name:_____

IP 925-3 • *Graphic Organizers for Math*
Copyright © 2007 by Incentive Publications, Inc., Nashville, TN.

BASIC CIRCLE GRAPH

Title:_____

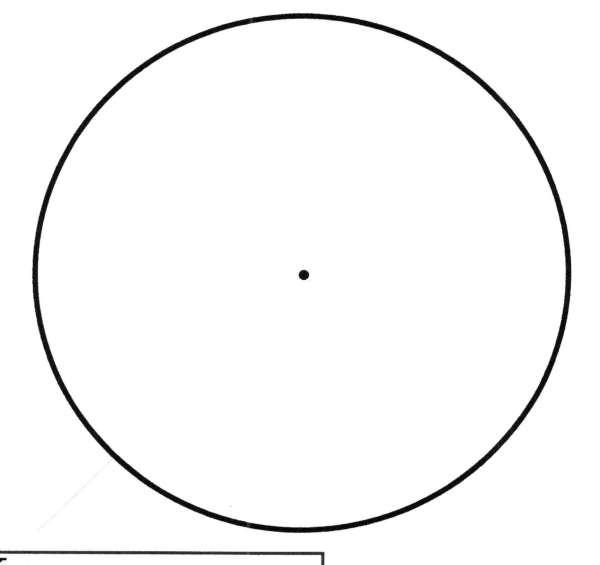

Key:

Name:_____

IP 925-3 • *Graphic Organizers for Math*
Copyright ©2007 by Incentive Publications, Inc., Nashville, TN.

Name: _____

Basic BAR Graph

Title: _____

Be sure to label
your graph!

IP 925-3 • *Graphic Organizers for Math*
Copyright © 2007 by Incentive Publications, Inc., Nashville, TN.

Be sure to label
your graph.

Basic  Graph

Title: _____

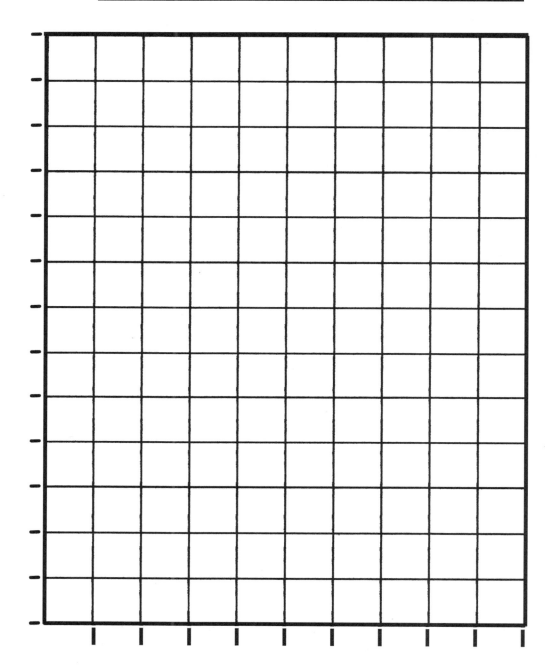

Key

Name: _____

BASIC PICTOGRAPH

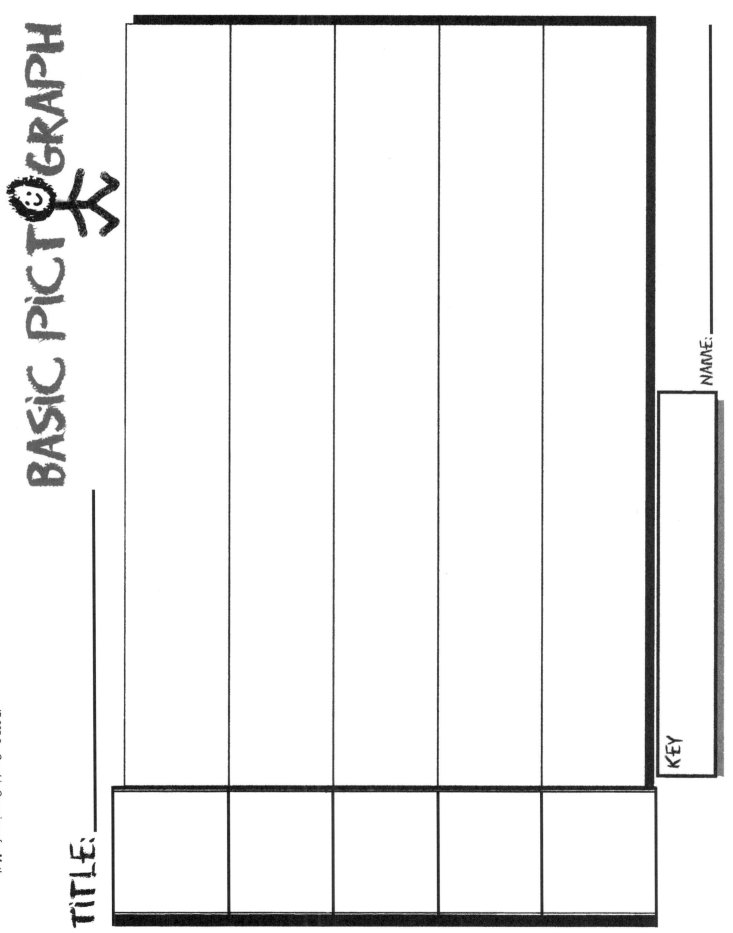

TITLE:

KEY

NAME:

IP 925-3 • Graphic Organizers for Math
Copyright ©2007 by Incentive Publications, Inc., Nashville, TN.

Tree Diagram

Outcomes or Combinations

Label: _____

Label: _____

Name: _____

IP 925-3 • *Graphic Organizers for Math*
Copyright © 2007 by Incentive Publications, Inc., Nashville, TN.

Basic Two–Quadrant Coordinate Grid

Name: _____

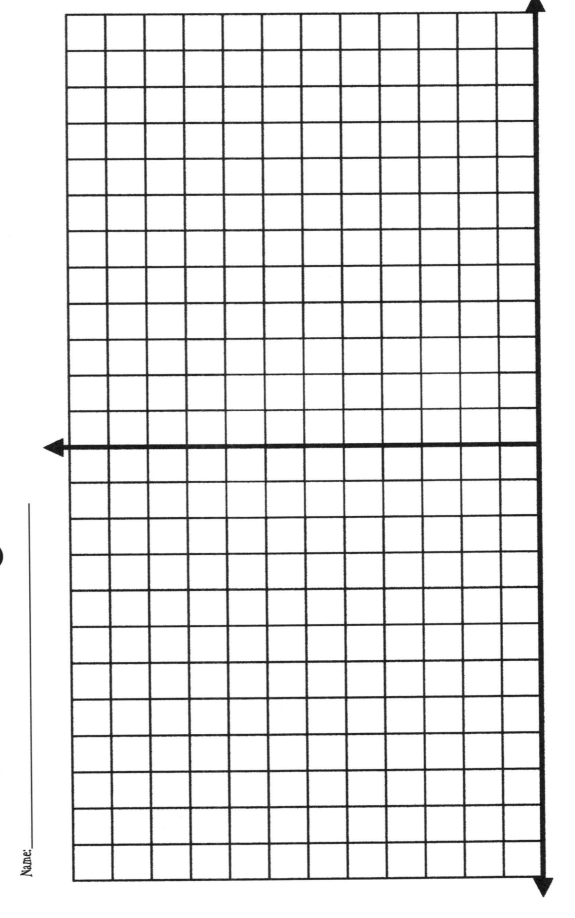

Add numbers to the grid.

IP 925-3 • *Graphic Organizers for Math*
Copyright © 2007 by Incentive Publications, Inc., Nashville, TN.

BASIC FOUR-QUADRANT COORDINATE GRID

Add numbers to the grid.

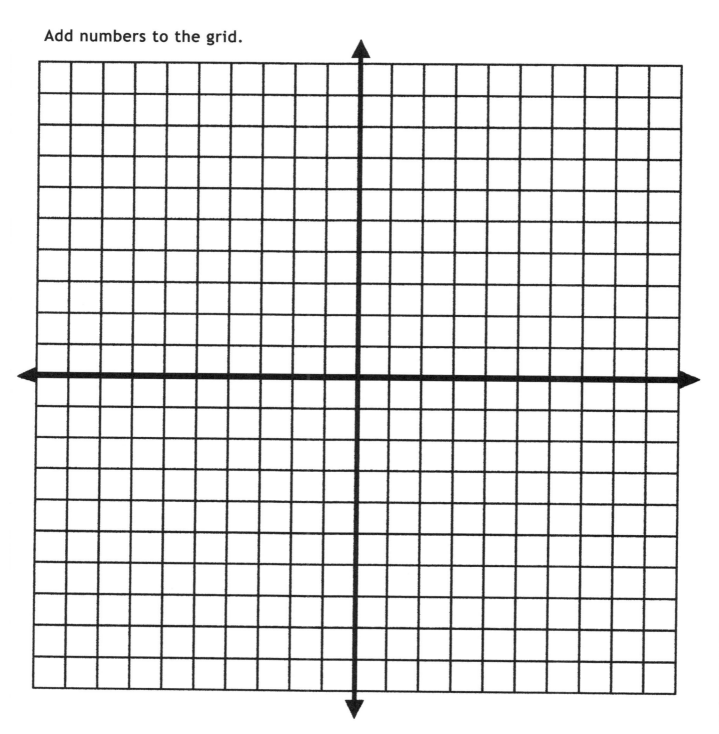

NAME:_____

IP 925-3 • *Graphic Organizers for Math*
Copyright ©2007 by Incentive Publications, Inc., Nashville, TN.

IP 925-3 • *Graphic Organizers for Math*

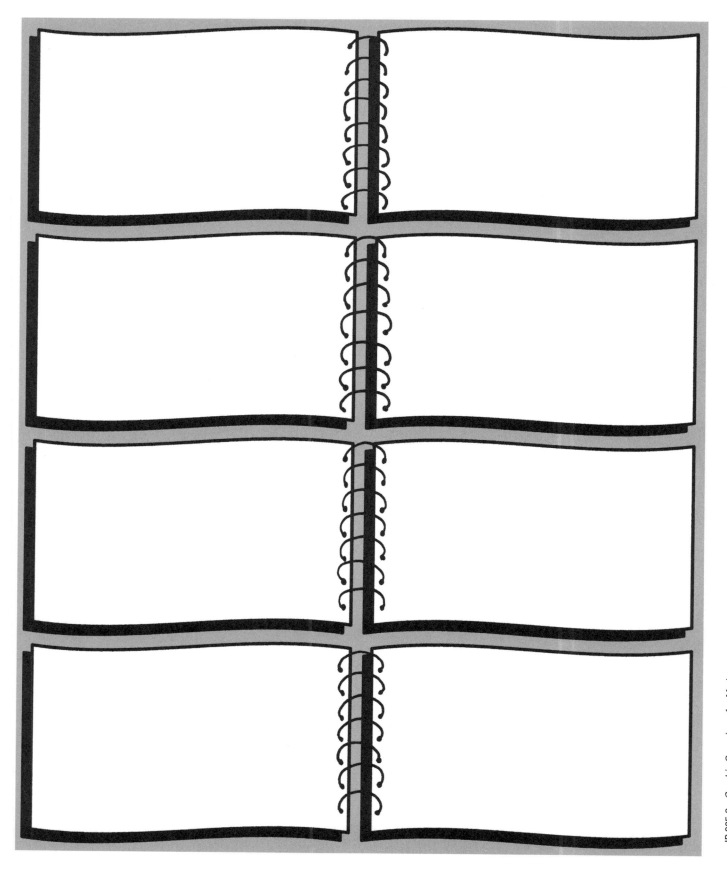

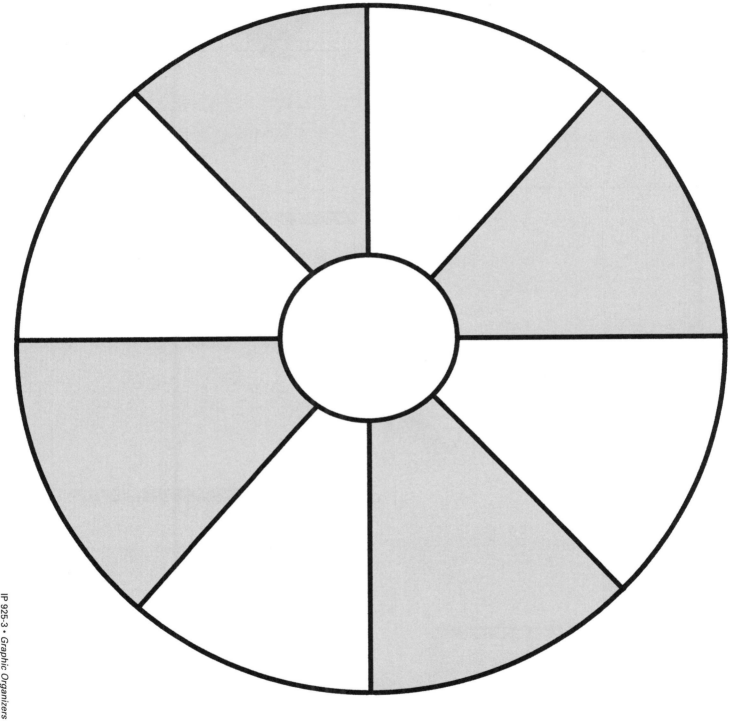

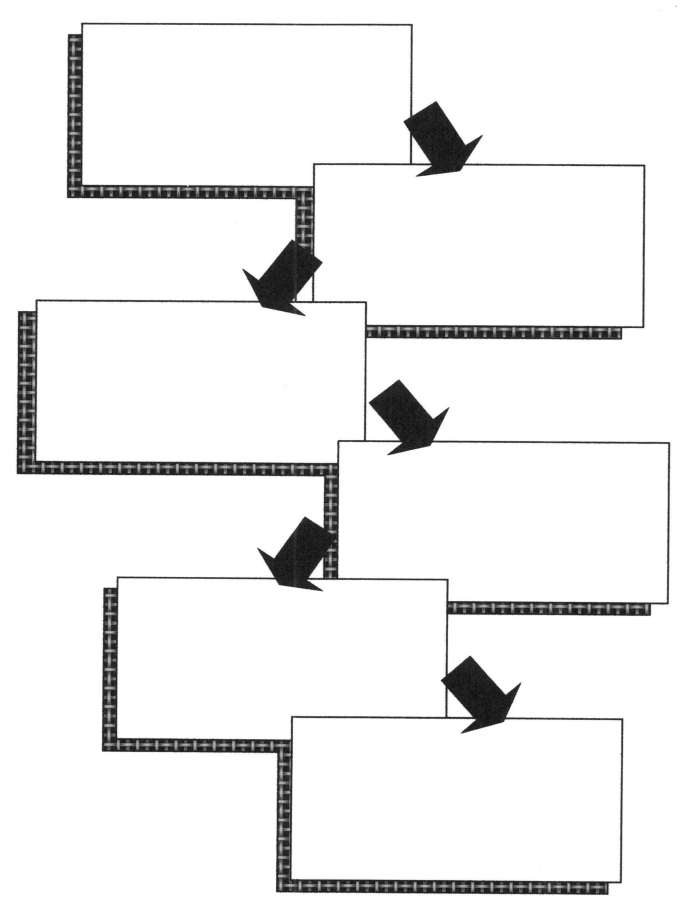